Children's Rooms

From Newborns to Teens

Tina Skinner
Melissa Cardona
Nathaniel Wolfgang-Price

Schiffer Publishing Ltd
4880 Lower Valley Road, Atglen, PA 19310 USA

Acknowledgments

We owe many thanks to Nate Wolfgang-Price, whose dedication, amazing capacity for writing, and willingness to work have proved invaluable to our team; to Paula Markowitz, for her informative essay regarding safety issues in the nursery; to Karen McNeill Harris and Young America® for their generous and beautiful contribution to the book; and finally, to all our contributors and their wonderful designs, without whom there would be no book!

Library of Congress Cataloging-in-Publication Data

Skinner, Tina.
Children's rooms : from newborns to teens / by Tina Skinner, Melissa Cardona, Nathaniel Wolfgang-Price.
p. cm.
ISBN 0-7643-2147-1 (pbk.)
1. Children's rooms. 2. Interior decoration.
I. Cardona, Melissa. II. Wolfgang-Price, Nathaniel.
III. Title.

NK2117.C4S577 2005
747.7'7—dc22

2004018225

Designed by "Sue"
Type set in CroissantD/Zurich BT

ISBN: 0-7643-2147-1
Printed in China

Editorial Team

Publisher: Peter Schiffer
Editorial Director: Tina Skinner
Editor: Melissa Cardona
Writers: Nathaniel Wolfgang-Price
Paula Markowitz
Melissa Cardona
Contents and Design Team Director: Sue Taltoan
Cover Design: John Cheek

Published by Schiffer Publishing Ltd.
4880 Lower Valley Road
Atglen, PA 19310
Phone: (610) 593-1777; Fax: (610) 593-2002
E-mail: Info@schifferbooks.com

For the largest selection of fine reference books on this and related subjects, please visit our web site at

www.schifferbooks.com

We are always looking for people to write books on new and related subjects. If you have an idea for a book please contact us at the above address.

This book may be purchased from the publisher.
Include $3.95 for shipping.
Please try your bookstore first.

You may write for a free catalog.

In Europe, Schiffer books are distributed by
Bushwood Books
6 Marksbury Ave.
Kew Gardens
Surrey TW9 4JF England
Phone: 44 (0) 20 8392-8585; Fax: 44 (0) 20 8392-9876
E-mail: info@bushwoodbooks.co.uk
Free postage in the U.K., Europe; air mail at cost.

CONTENTS

Introduction

It's time to redecorate your child's room, and as a parent, you want the best for your child! With the recent boom in retail products geared towards babies and children, however, the process of decorating for a child can be a daunting one. In addition to the usual home décor options in wallpaper, bedding, and furniture, there are now whole lines of products – at one time only available in adult sizes and motifs – made for little ones. This book is meant to give you an idea of what considerations to make in order to create a practical and special space for your child, help you sort through all the décor choices for your child's bedroom, and provide you with plenty of inspiration to start planning a wonderful sanctuary that your child will enjoy for years to come.

Sure, you want your child's room to look good, but no matter how old your child is, form should always follow function when planning his or her bedroom, particularly when purchasing furniture. Because furniture will most likely be the most expensive purchase you make, it's important to consider your child's future needs as well as his or her current ones. Similarly, you need to determine what's essential in the design of a room and what's just for show. Once you've determined what your child really needs, then you can start planning the color scheme, themes, and other decorative touches.

Designed for a baby girl, the simple pink and green furnishings provide a calm and cozy atmosphere. Headboards that were made into a day bed work as transitional pieces for the next stage of her life. *Courtesy of Christian Huebner Interiors, Inc.*

How a Baby Grows

When decorating your first child's nursery, you should definitely plan on purchasing a bassinet or cradle, a crib, a changing table, and a chest of drawers or some shelves. Your child will not sleep in a crib after the first couple years of life, and there are furniture manufacturers who offer cribs and parts that can easily be transformed into training beds and then beds for "big" girls and boys. A changing table can be substituted by a bookshelf or another piece of furniture – just as long as it's safe for your baby! You'll also want to consider your own needs and comfort in the nursery – an armchair, glider, or rocking chair is a definite must. Above all, the safety of your child should be your primary concern when planning a nursery, and an essay written by PatchKraft® president and child-safety advocate Paula Markowitz is included in this book to help inform you of some issues regarding your infant's safety in his or her nursery.

As she transitions into her "big girl" room, drapery and bedding fabrics carry the theme from her infant room. The day bed from the infant room is turned into headboards for the twin beds. *Courtesy of Christian Huebner Interiors, Inc.*

As your babies grow into toddlers and then begin attending school, they'll need more storage options in their rooms – especially for all those toys and books! Their clothes will also take up more room, so be sure to have a dresser, armoire, or shelves to store such necessities. A desk with a lamp is another item that you'll also need to consider. Homework can easily be done at the kitchen table, but it's a good idea to get kids in the habit of completing lessons in their own, private, designated space for such tasks. Most children are afraid of the dark, so you should include a bedside table with a lamp in your furniture purchases so they can turn a light on or off without venturing off into the dark unknown of their bedroom at night. A night table is also a good place to keep a journal, a book for reading, or a glass of water.

This crib grows with your child, providing a training bed, day bed, and a full-size bed all in one. Furnishings such as these make decorating easier, and less expensive. *Courtesy of Bonavita*

Once you figure out the furniture needs of your children's rooms, you can begin choosing between color schemes, themes, and other décor details. The primary thing to keep in mind when decorating your child's room is that his or her taste is likely to change rapidly in their growing years. While it's fun to decorate your children's rooms with their favorite cartoon characters, in this case you should prepare to redecorate in just a few, short years. Likewise, although your three-year-old daughter's favorite color may be hot pink, when she turns twelve she may find the color childish. It's important to start off with a simple and basic plan for the room's décor. You'll want basic colors that will appeal to your child as he or she matures. Items like bedding, curtains, and decorative accessories can be changed to reflect the child's changing tastes. Flexibility is an important element when planning for your child's space – so always keep the future in mind.

Of course, you're not the only one with a say in the décor of your child's room. Your children should have some say in what their rooms look like, so involve them in the process. If you've got young children, let them choose between a few color schemes that you've picked out. Flip through this book together to generate ideas and to see what your child finds attractive. Decorating your child's room should be fun, and it can be a good way to spend some time together.

We hope that this book fills you with lots of inspiration and that your child's room is a place that they'll enjoy well into the future!

Light blue walls and white bedclothes are ideal for a baby of either sex. A rocking chair is a must in any nursery. *Courtesy Young America®, A Division of Stanley Furniture Company, Inc.*

Preparing for Your First Infant

Pregnancy is a joyful time filled with the anticipation of a new life. The excitement of planning the nursery – your baby's nursery – is tempered by the exhaustion of the shopping, the choices, and, yes, the expenses of the final decisions. The information below will help you make some beautiful and informed decisions.

There are many questions and decisions regarding the design and décor of the nursery. The choice is yours as far as theme, style, color, and price. You may ask yourself, "What colors do I like? What style of bedding do I prefer? Do I want license characters, floral prints, genderless color schemes, patchwork?" There are so many choices and there is so much to do!

A beautiful nursery with all the trimmings is definitely a wonderful thing.

With all the beauty, however, there must come understanding, knowledge, and awareness of the safety issues that should be inherent in your decisions and choices of what to purchase for your baby's nursery. The bedding industry together with the Juvenile Products Manufacturers Association (www.jpma.org) and the American Society for Testing and Materials (www.astm.org) have been hard at work for several years creating and providing standards to help the consumer have the best information and options at their fingertips.

To start, bumpers are necessary. They have been used in cribs for generations. Considered an integral part of the crib's interior, they protect your baby from impact to his or her soft little head, and offer security along with definition of place. There are safety issues with bumpers that you should be aware of. Bumpers that are too thick, fluffy, or have a filling that is too loose can become a pillow in the crib – which is a definite no-no. You want a bumper that is, of course, a beautiful complement to the bedding set and to the crib, and one that is firm and has plenty of ties to hold it in place. This is very important so that your infant will not crawl underneath the bumper and get wedged in.

I personally recommend bumper ties for both the top and the bottom to provide total security. According to the present standard, bumper ties should be no longer than nine inches and no shorter than seven inches. This rule was passed in order to prevent strangulation in the crib from excessively long ties. Large ribbon ties form beautiful, fluffy bows on the end, but, sad to say, pose a risk to the baby.

While shopping, keep in mind that some cribs on the market today are not compatible for bumpers. These cribs may have solid end panels without slits where bumper ties should go. "Static," or "lifestyle" cribs that feature a stationary drop side also pose a safety issue. The problem with these are corner posts so thick that nine-inch long bumper ties cannot fit around them. Be sure to buy a crib that is beautiful, well made, and able to support your dream bedding set within the recommended safety guidelines.

Comforters, especially heavy and very thick comforters, should not be used in the crib with newborns. A lightweight blanket is perfect for the early months. There is plenty of time for babies to cuddle with comforters once they are able to pull themselves up and be more active in the crib.

Sheets must be well made in order to fit securely and hug the mattress. If the sheet is too tight when it is brand new, chances are it will shrink and not fit properly after the first wash. Sheets that are too big will also not fit properly. However, if you wash them before the first use, they will probably shrink to the proper size. If they don't, you should return them.

Mobiles are designed for newborns, but must be removed from the crib once an infant can pull himself or herself to a standing position. Here is a great decorating tip for your mobile: Attach some clear fish wire to the top of the hook and hang it from the ceiling somewhere away from the crib; across the room is a good place. This way, your precious baby will be entertained, your mobile will have a longer life, and the safety issue will be addressed. Wall hangings are beautiful, colorful, and certainly an important decorating tool in the nursery, but don't hang them over the crib where your curious little explorer could get into trouble.

There is a large variety of bedding choices on the market – your options in designs and materials are virtually endless. Many ensembles today are 100 percent cotton, but some sets require dry-cleaning. Some fabrications are cotton/poly blends that are also machine-washable and dryer-safe. The choice is yours. There are also fabrics on the market, such as chenille, which make beautiful bathrobes, blankets, and decorative throw pillows for the adult market, but which are not totally safe for infants because of the threads that pull out of them. These threads could easily end up in your baby's fingers and just as easily in baby's mouth, posing a serious gagging hazard.

Hopefully this information has helped to clarify some basic safety issues, as you are about to embark on a very special mission in your life. The more questions and information you have, the better and easier your decisions will be. Enjoy!

Paula Markowitz, President
PatchKraft®, Inc.

>
Baby's name hangs on the wall, and guarantees she'll know how to spell it in no time. *From the Waverly® Country House Collection*

<
Teddy bears on holiday cavort around shady oak trees on this wallpaper. The bright colors and playful pictures are suitable for any child's nursery. *From the Waverly® Storytime II Collection*

Natural wood coloring allows this furniture to blend in well with the color of the room. *Courtesy of Bonavita*

J.H.

<

Ship patterned fabric on the curtains and the chair adds a lighthearted air to this baby's nursery. *Courtesy of BNK Design Consultants*

A ceiling painted with clouds is a popular decorative choice for a baby's nursery, as the sky theme is suitable for toddlers and school age children as well. A comfy chair with ottoman gives mama and papa a place to rest while comforting baby, and is a must for any nursery. *Courtesy of Evelyn Benatar Interior Design*

<

In anticipation of a baby girl, this nursery was decorated in pink and white with lacy frills to give the furnishings a softer look. *Courtesy of One Step Ahead*

An infant's nursery should reflect the parents' taste, as they'll be spending plenty of time in their new baby's room. The attractive wallpaper and window treatments in this nursery will certainly appeal to this girl even as a teenager. *Courtesy of Evelyn Benatar Interior Design*

Walls and ceilings painted like the sky make the nursery feel open, and a sturdy, four-post crib makes the baby feel safe and snug. *Courtesy of Lisa Landry and Interiors by Decorating Den*

>

Pale green walls and friendly frogs are good company for a new baby. *Courtesy of KooKoo Bear Kids*

Circus themes are always popular for decorating nurseries and are suitable for both baby girls and boys. *Courtesy of PoshTots.com*

SEAN

A natural finish for a crib is a good choice for a baby boy. *Courtesy Young America®, A Division of Stanley Furniture Company, Inc.*

Yellow walls make a nursery seem sunnier, and a nursery rhyme border is suitable for a baby of either sex. *Courtesy of Eisenhart® Wallcoverings Co.*

Baby's
First
Bank
BABY
SLEEPIN

<
Teddy bears and pale green walls create an atmosphere of calm and security. *Courtesy of Eisenhart® Wallcoverings Co.*

This baby princess will surely never tire of her elegant and feminine surroundings. *Courtesy Young America®, A Division of Stanley Furniture Company, Inc.*

Yellow brings a hint of cheer into the nursery of a baby girl or boy. *Courtesy of KooKoo Bear Kids*

Checkered green and white is an excellent, soothing, gender neutral pattern and the ocean theme is appealing to either a baby boy or girl. *Courtesy of One Step Ahead*

This crib becomes the centerpiece of the room with the addition of dramatically draped fabric. *Courtesy of PoshTots.com*

A day bed converts into a crib when baby outgrows a bassinet. Teddy bears provide cheerful company when mom's away. *Courtesy of PoshTots.com*

In a perfectly designed bedroom featuring a soft pink and sage color scheme, this patchwork nursery rhyme motif and all the accessories coordinate to match the beautiful pastel design. *Courtesy of PatchKraft®*

All's right in the heavens and here on earth in this beautiful and comforting celestial theme in soft pastels. The patchwork design is perfect for either a girl or a boy. *Courtesy of PatchKraft®*

Curving lines and intricate carvings make this furniture decorative and give the nursery a beautiful, classic décor. *Courtesy of Bonavita*

Colorful bedding and a throw rug brighten up a gray room. *Courtesy Young America®, A Division of Stanley Furniture Company, Inc.*

Every day is a day at the circus in this room, with carnival themed wallpaper designed to appeal to the young and the young at heart. A crib and daybed in the room allow mom to nap alongside baby. *Courtesy of Thibaut®*

Photography by Lucia Herrera

>

This wallpaper features a border of birdhouses on both the top and the bottom, suggesting the atmosphere of a country garden. *From the Waverly® Storytime II Collection*

This room was designed with natural materials to be safe, environmentally friendly, and allergy free. A spacious wall unit can be converted from a changing table and cabinet to a desk and TV closet to accommodate children as they grow. *Courtesy of Theresa Russel Interiors*

Clouds and seagulls fly above a sleigh crib, lulling a baby to sleep like the rhythmic crashing of waves. The far wall of the nursery is covered in characters from Noah's Ark, and a blue and white plaid window treatment dresses the window. *Courtesy of KAT Interiors Group, Inc.*

Toddlers

For The Girls

A picket fence headboard makes this room feel like a garden. Hula-hoops make a unique decorative feature. *Courtesy of Fashion Kids*

Yellow and bright green create a rather vivid color scheme, while a child's name adds a personal touch to please a younger girl. A colorful and ornate light fixture enhances the vibrant room. *Courtesy of PoshTots.com*

A mural of a child reading framed on either side by yellow and white striped pillars give this room a picture book theme, while the ceiling gives the child the feeling she is sleeping under the sky. *Courtesy of Buena Vista Faux & Mural Painting*

<
This bunk bed configuration allows the sleeper to feel she has more room and has space for a small bedside table. *Courtesy Young America®, A Division of Stanley Furniture Company, Inc.*

Turned the other way, this bunk bed offers drawers with space for clothes or extra blankets. *Courtesy Young America®, A Division of Stanley Furniture Company, Inc.*

Light pink and green bedclothes create a springtime atmosphere in this little girl's room. *Courtesy Young America®, A Division of Stanley Furniture Company, Inc.*

Playtime never ends with beds and other furniture accessories covered by tent-like roofs. A vivid color scheme and a fun fish-covered border add to this room's playfulness. *Courtesy of Bambini Design*

Wildflowers and soft fabrics make for sweet dreams. *Courtesy of PoshTots.com*

A bed with rails on the sides makes this little girl feel like a "big girl," but still keeps her safe. *Courtesy Young America®, A Division of Stanley Furniture Company, Inc.*

Decorated for a little princess, this room features lacy curtains and ornate furniture straight out of a fairytale. *Courtesy of PoshTots.com*

<
Fairy tales do come true in this room, but kids should be sure to fall asleep before midnight lest the bed turn back into a pumpkin! *Courtesy of PoshTots.com*

This four-post bed is hung with curtains to ensure a child sleeps in peace. *Courtesy of Fashion Kids*

Thin slats are spaced to meet safety standards while allowing plenty of light into this set of bunk beds. *Courtesy Young America®, A Division of Stanley Furniture Company, Inc.*

<
A pink and purple canopy covers a pretty lilac bed. *Courtesy of One Step Ahead*

A white wicker headboard is the perfect choice for a little girl's room filled with beautiful, warm, and charming floral patterns that will suit her style as she grows older. *Courtesy of PatchKraft®*

<

Headboard, lampshade, and a bench at the end of the bed add décor in a powdery pink room. *Courtesy Young America®, A Division of Stanley Furniture Company, Inc.*

A string of your child's favorite snapshots makes a creative, personal, and inexpensive decorative element. *Courtesy of Moosehead Mfg. Co.*

A throw rug on wood floors designates a softer playtime space for children. *Courtesy of Moosehead Mfg. Co.*

This room is filled with feminine furnishings that will grow up with this little girl. Broad white and yellow stripes and blue, sky-like walls are separated by a pretty ballerina-studded border. *Courtesy of Hillner-Browne Interior Design, L.L.C.*

Drawers built into the bottom of this bed offer a convenient solution to any storage problem. *Courtesy Young America®, A Division of Stanley Furniture Company, Inc.*

Rabbits are the theme of this room, which seems to come straight out of the pages of a storybook. Rich pink and green fabrics and storybook pictures are certain to appeal to a younger girl. *Courtesy of PoshTots.com*

A furniture set can be mixed and matched. Dark colored chest of drawers and shelves provide an attractive contrast in a light colored room. *Courtesy of Moosehead Mfg. Co.*

This bedroom has plenty of roommates, with shelving that makes space for them all. *Courtesy of Lexington Home Brands*

A hot pink blanket and window valences along with electric blue curtains against bright yellow walls combine to form a brilliant color scheme. *Courtesy of Suzanne Price and Interiors by Decorating Den*

The imagination is inspired by the beautiful pictorial toile quilt. Soft peachy pink accents in the neutral colored room add just enough femininity without overwhelming the senses. *Courtesy of PatchKraft®*

A simple wrought iron frame allows this bed to stay with this girl while she matures. Curtain shears add whimsy and wonder to the boldly painted walls. *Courtesy of Fashion Kids*

Teddy bears always make a room feel welcoming and look more kid-friendly. *Courtesy of Moosehead Mfg. Co.*

This room brings the outdoors inside. Just like a storybook garden, cloth flowers bloom beside the bed and on the blankets, and trees grow on the walls. A quilt-like valance in primary colors is another unique touch. *Courtesy of Jan Tomlinson and Interiors by Decorating Den*

Strings of colorful plastic rings replace those boring old curtains. Beanbag chairs and large cushions make perfect seats for little ones. *Courtesy Young America®, A Division of Stanley Furniture Company, Inc.*

Lilac is the perfect color for any girl's room. An area rug was embellished by placing two decorative throw rugs on top of it. *Courtesy Young America®, A Division of Stanley Furniture Company, Inc.*

Flower power creates a lively and fun atmosphere in this room. *Courtesy Young America®, A Division of Stanley Furniture Company, Inc.*

This bed makes a perfect place for story time. *Courtesy Young America®, A Division of Stanley Furniture Company, Inc.*

>

Plenty of hearts for a little sweetheart. A cushioned window seat provides a great place for children to curl up, and storage space underneath for when they clean up. *Courtesy of Eisenhart® Wallcoverings Co.*

Green fabric draped over the posts of a bed add elegance and sophistication to this little girl's room. *Courtesy of Fashion Kids*

Sometimes simplicity is best, with a plain wrought iron frame suitable for a princess of any age. *Courtesy of Fashion Kids*

Photography by Edward Purcell

Photography by Edward Purcell

Dreams come alive in this room, where playful fairies cavort on the walls. The pale blues and gauzy whites create a soothing and calm atmosphere, while the antique furniture and dried flowers bring the dreamer back to earth. *Courtesy of Lisa Johnson, ASID*

Dress up is the theme for this bedroom's wallcoverings. Lively pastel colors on a light rose background make a combination ideal for a little girl who loves to try on pretty dresses. *From the Waverly Storytime II Collection*

Dark furnishings inhabit a brightly-painted room, which harbors all kinds of childhood adventures. *Courtesy of Fashion Kids*

Photography by David Durbak

Bright pastels and hearts create a cheerful atmosphere just right for a little sweetheart. *Courtesy of Theresa Russel Interiors*

Photography by David Durbak

Bows are the main theme of this room, and the color purple makes it perfect for any little princess. *Courtesy of Theresa Russel Interiors*

Automobiles are the theme of this room. Bright colors make it a fun place to fall asleep and an exciting place to play. *Courtesy of Moosehead Mfg. Co.*

Off we go into the wild blue yonder. Planes ranging from WWII bombers to fighter jets fly on the ceiling, walls, floors, and the bed in this room belonging to a future ace. *Courtesy of Company Kids®*

A little boy's nautical adventure begins in his bedroom where he finds inspiration in the theme of the set, the coordinating wallpaper border, armchair, and assorted décor items. *Courtesy of PatchKraft®*

At the end of the trail, a room decorated in blue and red is perfect for sleeping under the stars. *Courtesy of Eisenhart® Wallcoverings Co.*

Dr. Livingston, I presume? The walls and ceilings in this room are painted to resemble a grass hut, while a giraffe and an elephant bring all the fun and excitement of an African Safari indoors. *Courtesy of Buena Vista Faux & Mural Painting*

Red bunk beds, a blue armchair, and stars on the walls give this room a patriotic feel. *Courtesy of Bassett Furniture*

A railing along its side and playful pillows make this bed a good choice in the first step from crib to a regular bed. *Courtesy Young America®, A Division of Stanley Furniture Company, Inc.*

Red, white, and blue feature prominently in this room. Plaid pillows and a plaid toy chest with the child's name quilted on the top add a touch of whimsy. "Things that go" is the main theme as evidenced by the custom bedspreads and the antique French posters on the wall. *Courtesy of Christian Huebner Interiors, Inc.*

'Tweens and Teens

Young Ladies

Paintings in this room are hung at the child's eye level, as well as bunk level. A hamper in the room ensures that clothes don't end up on the floor, and a desk provides a private place for study. *Courtesy Young America®, A Division of Stanley Furniture Company, Inc.*

White and blue are the primary colors in this room, with its air of cool simplicity. The flower print on the pillows and chair add a feminine touch that makes this room suitable for a young girl through teenage years. *Courtesy of Christian Huebner Interiors, Inc.*

Bold blue walls are offset by white furniture and one wall whose top half is painted white. A green throw rug and other accessories add color accents. *Courtesy Young America®, A Division of Stanley Furniture Company, Inc.*

Simply designed furniture is suitable for an older girl, who wants to keep her room looking nice, but not too frilly. A lava lamp and other lighting make cool decorative accents. *Courtesy Young America®, A Division of Stanley Furniture Company, Inc.*

A pink and green wall unit provides shelves for storage and a space for studying. *Courtesy of Melissa Arnold and Interiors by Decorating Den*

This bed has room to sleep a spare, a roll away bed, ideal for any sleepover. *Courtesy of Fashion Kids*

A day bed can serve as a couch or a place to sleep in a crowded bedroom. *Courtesy Young America®, A Division of Stanley Furniture Company, Inc.*

A day on the town is the theme for this border. Sophisticated young ladies would love these wallcoverings. *From the Village® Borders for All Around the House Collection*

Pink curtains are always a pretty touch. *Courtesy Young America®, A Division of Stanley Furniture Company, Inc.*

Carved footboards make pretty decorations for this girl's room, as do the broad pink and white stripes on the wall. *Courtesy Young America®, A Division of Stanley Furniture Company, Inc.*

This slatted sleigh bed comes with a trundle bed in case of unexpected sleepovers. Mixing and matching a child's favorite colors makes for a cozy décor statement. *Courtesy of Bassett Furniture*

A bright pastel quilt makes this room feel welcoming and makes it look fun. *Courtesy of Moosehead Mfg. Co.*

A night table with drawers offers this girl a convenient place to put her telephone and journal. *Courtesy Young America®, A Division of Stanley Furniture Company, Inc.*

>
On the wall in this room, a door leads to an imaginary garden. Dried flowers and floral prints bring that garden inside and keep springtime in the room even when it's snowing outside. *Courtesy of Bonnie Pressley and Interiors by Decorating Den*

An elegant bed is perfect for a girl who wants to feel all grown-up. *Courtesy Young America®, A Division of Stanley Furniture Company, Inc.*

>
A skylight brings plenty of light into this attic room, while streamlined furniture allows plenty of space for playing, hanging out, or doing homework. *Courtesy of Gautier USA, Inc*

Bold blue bedding and other bright accents liven up this white bedroom.
Courtesy Young America®, A Division of Stanley Furniture Company, Inc.

Thin, vertical pink stripes add interest to a light blue room. *Courtesy Young America®, A Division of Stanley Furniture Company, Inc.*

On matching beds, decorative pillows can add a personal touch. *Courtesy Young America®, A Division of Stanley Furniture Company, Inc.*

>
Bold pink walls and a feminine bed frame are perfect décor choices for girls who grow up quickly. *Courtesy of Fashion Kids*

A few pieces of furniture make rearranging the room easier. Blue stenciling above the window complements the bedding and rug. *Courtesy Young America®, A Division of Stanley Furniture Company, Inc.*

Pink poodles and black-and-white plaid give this girl's room an air of urban sophistication. *Courtesy of KooKoo Bear Kids*

>

Zany striped sheets add some color to these plain wooden bunk beds. Strings of colored lights against the wall add even more vibrancy to the room. *Courtesy Young America®, A Division of Stanley Furniture Company, Inc.*

Curtains on four-poster beds give children privacy when they sleep and add airiness to the room. *Courtesy Young America®, A Division of Stanley Furniture Company, Inc.*

>

White daisies on the wall bring a touch of spring inside and match well with white furniture. *Courtesy Young America®, A Division of Stanley Furniture Company, Inc.*

This room was designed to incorporate a few of an older girl's favorite things: the color blue, white wicker furniture, checks, and stripes. All of these things combine to create a room that is feminine but still sporty. *Courtesy of Lark Interiors*

©2004 Barry Halkin

There is plenty of monkey business going on in this room. Monkeys are the primary theme with music as a secondary one. Green walls and pink highlights make this room perfect for a little girl. *Courtesy of Lark Interiors*

Curtains hung on a canopy bed will make any little girl feel like a princess. *Courtesy of KooKoo Bear Kids*

>

Pink is perfect for a little girl. *Courtesy Young America®, A Division of Stanley Furniture Company, Inc.*

Kaitlyn
Kaitlyn

<

Flowers, stars, and a bright yellow bedspread light up this little girl's room, making it a great place to hang out with her friends. The custom border with her name makes her feel very special. *Courtesy of Eisenhart® Wallcoverings Co.*

Patchwork quilts can add a homey touch to a new room. *Courtesy Young America®, A Division of Stanley Furniture Company, Inc.*

Light green bedclothes and pale lilac walls create a soothing natural atmosphere. *Courtesy Young America®, A Division of Stanley Furniture Company, Inc.*

Lots of shelving helps sisters keep clutter to a minimum. *Courtesy Young America®, A Division of Stanley Furniture Company, Inc.*

<
A bright yellow canopy goes well with light purple walls and gives this girl a special place to hide away. *Courtesy of Bassett Furniture*

Full length and vanity mirrors make this room suitable for a girl of any age. *Courtesy Young America®, A Division of Stanley Furniture Company, Inc.*

Bedding with bright stripes adds a splash of color to a white room. *Courtesy Young America®, A Division of Stanley Furniture Company, Inc.*

<
Solid and bold, this yellow bedspread adds punch to an otherwise mild room. A light fixture above the bed allows this child to read at night, without having to brave the dark when it's time for lights out. *Courtesy of Fashion Kids*

A chest in the window can also serve as a window seat. *Courtesy Young America®, A Division of Stanley Furniture Company, Inc.*

Bedside shelves allow important things to be stored close at hand. *Courtesy Young America®, A Division of Stanley Furniture Company, Inc.*

A pink floral bedspread adds a splash of color to a plain white room. *Courtesy Young America®, A Division of Stanley Furniture Company, Inc.*

A curvy metal frame complete with ornamental knobs gives this particular bed an air of vintage elegance, while brightly colored walls and comforter create a lively atmosphere for a young girl or woman. *Courtesy of Fashion Kids*

>

Furniture placed close together makes a room feel cozier. *Courtesy Young America®, A Division of Stanley Furniture Company, Inc.*

Hand painted dragonflies and butterflies that glide across violet walls match this young lady's hand painted bedspread. Decorative chenille pillows on the bed coordinate with the cozy armchair. A shelf runs along the length of the room, placed high to display a collection of cherished books and other decorative items that are used infrequently. *Courtesy of Jan Kyle Design* V

>

This room will encourage monkey business with palm tress and a primate on the wall. A window seat creates a snug nook to curl up in. *Courtesy of Connie Thompson and Interiors by Decorating Den*

Pink and green is a popular color combination for young girls. *Courtesy of KooKoo Bear Kids*

A set of blue and pink bedding matches nicely with a blue and pink candy stripe pattern on the walls. *Courtesy Young America®, A Division of Stanley Furniture Company, Inc.*

A solid purple area rug protects the wooden floors from the kids while adding some color to the room. Bunk beds give siblings the space they need. *Courtesy Young America®, A Division of Stanley Furniture Company, Inc.*

Snug up under the eaves, this bed is sure to get plenty of sunlight. *Courtesy Young America®, A Division of Stanley Furniture Company, Inc.*

Patterned quilts provide an excellent way of adding color to any room.
Courtesy Young America®, A Division of Stanley Furniture Company, Inc.

A simple pine frame adds a touch of elegance to the room of any child. *Courtesy of Fashion Kids*

Cloth draped above the daybed adds elegance and vertical interest in this little girl's room. *Courtesy of Alan Nugent and Interiors by Decorating Den*

A girl's room finished with antiques makes this her feel like a princess.
Courtesy of Rebecca Shearn and Interiors by Decorating Den

Paper dolls are great toys for little girls, and in this room, they're even better decorations. *Courtesy of KooKoo Bear Kids*

<

A hand woven rug makes a nice compliment to a blue quilt, while green accents add some punch. *Courtesy Young America®, A Division of Stanley Furniture Company, Inc.*

>

A potted flower by the bed makes this light-colored room seem a little more cheerful. *Courtesy of Lexington Home Brands*

Light colored bedclothes combined with pale walls create a soothing haven for an excitable child. *Courtesy Young America®, A Division of Stanley Furniture Company, Inc.*

A large bed gives an older child room to stretch out. *Courtesy Young America®, A Division of Stanley Furniture Company, Inc.*

>

A bed frame with fabric-covered head and footboards adds décor to the room. *Courtesy Young America®, A Division of Stanley Furniture Company, Inc.*

Bunk beds aren't just for boys. Carved footboards make this configuration suitable for girls, too. *Courtesy Young America®, A Division of Stanley Furniture Company, Inc.*

A small mirror gives this bed a unique and old-fashioned look. *Courtesy of BNK Design Consultants*

>
A roll away bed gives extra space to this small room. *Courtesy of Lexington Home Brands*

With its sleek design, this wall-mounted vanity is a modern version of a feminine tradition. Hanging textiles play a major role in this room, where traditional and modern styling are mixed to form the perfect combination for a girl in her transitional years from girl to woman. *Courtesy of Bambini Design*

Young Men

>
Additional headroom on the bottom bunk provides extra space for a growing boy. *Courtesy Young America®, A Division of Stanley Furniture Company, Inc.*

Streamlined shelving is simple enough to suit an older boy. A gray and blue color scheme makes a cool impression on his friends. *Courtesy Young America®, A Division of Stanley Furniture Company, Inc.*

>
This young ranger's bedroom comes with bunk beds for those nights when he's not so lonely. Striped wallpaper makes a nice accompaniment to the cowboy themed wallpaper, and can be left there when the cowboy wants another theme for his room. *From the Waverly® Storytime II Collection*

This loft bed with shelves and drawers built into the unit offers a unique solution to any space problem. *Courtesy of Bassett Furniture*

Bright white and cool blue give this techie's room a futuristic look. *Courtesy of Gautier USA, Inc*

This bunk bed configuration makes a "cave" with room for a reading lamp on the bottom bunk. *Courtesy Young America®, A Division of Stanley Furniture Company, Inc.*

Bright yellow walls set apart by white ones add interest without being overwhelming. These modern furnishings will suit any child, even when they're in college. *Courtesy of Gautier USA, Inc*

This child's affinity for the outdoors is evidenced in his room's décor. *Courtesy Young America®, A Division of Stanley Furniture Company, Inc.*

A boy doesn't want a lot of clothing, and drawers built into his bed leave him room for more important things. *Courtesy Young America®, A Division of Stanley Furniture Company, Inc.*

>

A throw rug covered in thin stripes makes a small room seem larger. *Courtesy Young America®, A Division of Stanley Furniture Company, Inc.*

35
M.P.H.
EASTPAK

Blue plaid bedding offers a pattern that grows with a boy as he matures. Personalized monograms on his pillows really make him feel special. *Courtesy of KooKoo Bear Kids*

A gingham rug matches nicely with a dark blue bunk bed/futon combination. A basket bedside is an inexpensive and attractive storage option. *Courtesy Young America®, A Division of Stanley Furniture Company, Inc.*

This room provides a great place for an aspiring musician to practice. *Courtesy of Moosehead Mfg. Co.*

A telescope and pictures of celestial bodies on the wall reveal the hobby of this room's occupant. *Courtesy Young America®, A Division of Stanley Furniture Company, Inc.*

<

An alcove can give a bedroom a lot of extra space for an older child's things. *Courtesy of Lexington Home Brands*

It's not hard to guess what this boy's doing on Saturday. Sports decorations reflect this future varsity star's favorite pastimes. *Courtesy of KooKoo Bear Kids*

<
A tan-and-beige checked throw rug allows an infinite number of color scheme choices for a room's bedding and décor items. *Courtesy Young America®, A Division of Stanley Furniture Company, Inc.*

The same room in a different color scheme has a completely different character. Lots of shelving reduces the amount of clutter on the floor. *Courtesy Young America®, A Division of Stanley Furniture Company, Inc.*

<

Darker colors give a masculine feel to the room. A couch on the bottom of this set of bunk beds makes the most of the space available. *Courtesy Young America®, A Division of Stanley Furniture Company, Inc.*

This set of bunk beds provides extra space in a small room. Drawers in the ladder and a shelf built into the bed create plenty of storage, while two rollaway beds provide lots of room for a boy and his buddies. *Courtesy of Gautier USA, Inc*

<
The bigger the space, the more stuff you find to fill it. Lots of storage options keep the clutter at bay. *Courtesy Young America®, A Division of Stanley Furniture Company, Inc.*

Weekly Reader
MIDWAY
MIDWAY
MIDWAY
United States

<
An airplane border flies through a room filled with clouds, while a telescope keeps an eye on the sky. *Courtesy of Eisenhart® Wallcoverings Co.*

Boys always say they never collect too much stuff. A wall-unit desk combination offers plenty of shelf-space, just in case. *Courtesy Young America®, A Division of Stanley Furniture Company, Inc.*

The drawers beneath his bed give this boy a place to keep a few of his favorite things. *Courtesy Young America®, A Division of Stanley Furniture Company, Inc.*

A shelf built into the headboard means that important toys are always close by, and a roll-away bed is just waiting for a friend to spend the night. *Courtesy of Lexington Home Brands*

A custom border and striped sheets add color to this boy's room. *Courtesy of Eisenhart® Wallcoverings Co.*

Guestrooms

The simplicity of the white stars on a mottled blue and white background gives this room a country air with a slightly patriotic feel. *From the Waverly® Country House Collection*

Colorful country quilts sit folded and waiting for a cold winter's night. *Courtesy of Lexington Home Brands*

>
This rodeo themed bedding is a great choice for those future cowboys and cowgirls. *Courtesy of Aubergine Home Collection, Inc.*

With two roll-away beds, this room is more than ready for any sleepover at grandpa's. *Courtesy of Lexington Home Brands*

Rodeo

<
Toile wallpaper adds a touch of sophistication to this room, steeped in traditions and perfect for any child or an older guest. *Courtesy of Thibaut®*

>
A couch for friends when they come over, and a pull-out bed for when they stay. *Courtesy Young America®, A Division of Stanley Furniture Company, Inc.*

When the grandkids come for an extended stay, a laundry basket at the foot of the bed ensures dirty clothes won't end up on the floor. *Courtesy Young America®, A Division of Stanley Furniture Company, Inc.*

<
Cotton bedding in soft, pastel colors creates a feminine atmosphere perfect for a little girl who one day dreams of being a princess. *Courtesy of Aubergine Home Collection, Inc.*

Floral wallpaper and border on an off-white background lends this room a calm air. F*rom the Village® Artistic Flair Collection*

Butterflies on a yellow background create a bright springtime air that lights up the room, making it suitable for a younger girl. *From the Waverly® Storytime II Collection*

>

Bunnies hop around the walls and wait on the bed in a room decorated in white and soft pink. The classic décor will make young guests feel all grown up. *Courtesy of Eisenhart® Wallcoverings Co.*

Flowers on a yellow background beneath a light green plaid pattern make this room seem much brighter and bring forth a country springtime atmosphere suitable for a girl who appreciates the simple things in life. *From the Growing Up with Waverly® Collection*

Peach colored walls and light furnishings make this room seem even brighter. *Courtesy of Lexington Home Brands*

A yellow and blue canopy incorporates the window treatment and makes this sleigh bed the centerpiece of the room. *Courtesy of BNK Design Consultants*

Victorian style furnishings make this room ideal for a sophisticated older girl. *Courtesy of Lexington Home Brands.*

Done in green and purple, this room recreates a natural atmosphere, which is enhanced by dried flowers wound around the canopy of a wrought iron bed and flowers stenciled on the walls. *Courtesy of Susan Comfort and Interiors by Decorating Den*

Blue and yellow bedding add color to a white room. A chest at the foot of the bed makes a space for clothes and extra sheets, or secret treasures. *Courtesy of Lexington Home Brands*

<

Twin beds with roses on the footboards fit very well into a guestroom. *Courtesy of Rebecca Shearn and Interiors by Decorating Den*

Placing some of your grandchildren's favorite toys in a guestroom automatically transforms it into their space. *Courtesy of Fashion Kids*

A step-stool is useful if a little girl will sleep in a big bed while visiting her grandparents' house. A string of dried flowers above the window adds decorative flair. *Courtesy of Lexington Home Brands*

A green bed and blue and tan furniture add a bit of "Joy" to this room. *Courtesy of Bassett Furniture*

Curtain sheers match the decorative pillows on the bed, and decorative wall hangings support the green and lilac color scheme of the room. *Courtesy Young America®, A Division of Stanley Furniture Company, Inc.*

Twin beds are suitable for children who must share a room. A decorative rug in the shape of a flower adds décor to an otherwise sparely decorated room. *Courtesy Young America®, A Division of Stanley Furniture Company, Inc.*

<

Tucked up under the eaves, the subtle coloration of the wallpaper creates a calm atmosphere suitable for a child visiting grandma's house, or for any of her other guests. *Courtesy of Thibaut®*

A couch by day, this day bed can sleep two with the pull-out bed underneath. In this attic room, where space is limited, a wall was built against the eaves to create a shelf for extra storage and display space. *Courtesy Young America®, A Division of Stanley Furniture Company, Inc.*

A color scheme rich in mauves and greens is appropriate for young girls and young ladies, as are the floral and plaid patterns that inhabit this room. *Courtesy of PatchKraft®*

These twin beds can be debunked as children grow up, or left just so to conserve space. *Courtesy of Fashion Kids*

This collapsible cot provides some extra space for extra guests. *Courtesy Young America®, A Division of Stanley Furniture Company, Inc.*

An antique iron and brass bed painted white compliments a light floral pattern and gives the room a feminine sensibility. *Courtesy of Culpepper-Taylor Design*

A child is surrounded by his favorite things, like automobiles and animals, with the colorful choice of décor items. *Courtesy Young America®, A Division of Stanley Furniture Company, Inc.*

Rooms in Vacations Homes

Photography by www.jayrosenblatt.com

Photography by www.jayrosenblatt.com

This room was designed for a small boy who loves summer visits to his grandfather's home on the coast of Maine. Wall murals set the scene for this boy's adventures from shore to sea, and a sailboat bed ensures his seafaring journeys continue through the night. *Courtesy of Diane Boyer, ASID*

Photography by Dennis Welsh

> A carved headboard adds a little decoration to a plain country cottage room. *Courtesy of Maine Cottage*

A small bed with drawers on the bottom makes the most of the space in an attic room. *Courtesy Young America®, A Division of Stanley Furniture Company, Inc.*

Dark furnishings add contrast in a light room, and will serve children well as they get older. *Courtesy Young America®, A Division of Stanley Furniture Company, Inc.*

>
A slightly wider bottom bunk gives an older child plenty of room, while a younger child can sleep on the top.
Courtesy Young America®, A Division of Stanley Furniture Company, Inc.

Storage beneath the bed is a convenient place to stash toys when cleaning up.
Courtesy Young America®, A Division of Stanley Furniture Company, Inc.

Bedspreads and rugs add a colorful touch to any room and can be easily replaced as a child's taste changes. *Courtesy of Lexington Home Brands*

Photography by Dennis Welsh

>
Red and blue add a patriotic flair to a weekend retreat. *Courtesy of Maine Cottage*

Light blue finish on the bed and bedside table go along well with a plain white room. *Courtesy of Bassett Furniture*

A simple wooden frame without any carvings appeals to an older boy. *Courtesy Young America®, A Division of Stanley Furniture Company, Inc.*

Bright white and cool blue give this surfer's room just the right feel. Waves on the wall mean he's never far from where the action is. *Courtesy of Gautier USA, Inc*

A wave border on the wall and boats on the blankets bring the beach indoors. *Courtesy Young America®, A Division of Stanley Furniture Company, Inc.*

Ahoy mates, 'tis the sailor's life for this room. This sailing ship mural creates the illusion that the child is sleeping on the deck of his own ship bound for the high seas. *Courtesy of Buena Vista Faux & Mural Painting*

Deep blue and sand colored walls make an excellent color scheme for a room at the shore. *Courtesy of Seaman's Kids*

Photography by Dennis Welsh

Bunk beds fit quite nicely into a little cabin in the woods. *Courtesy of Maine Cottage*

This guestroom with cozy furnishings and bedding could make any child feel right at home. *Courtesy of Lexington Home Brands*

A blue plush armchair adds an extra bit of comfort to this little sailor's room. *Courtesy of Bassett Furniture*

Natural wood finish provides an excellent match to hard wood floors. A mirror with corkboard sides provides a great solution to your child's desire to use tape. *Courtesy of Bassett Furniture*

Plain wooden frames give a sturdy look to these beds for siblings. Chalkboards above the bed allow the kids to create their own décor. *Courtesy of Fashion Kids*

Playrooms

Cars and trucks race around the border of this playroom, a theme which is always popular with younger boys. *Courtesy of Eisenhart® Wallcoverings Co.*

Frogs hop along the walls and curtains of this room, where children's play is limited only by the imagination. *From the Waverly Storytime II Collection*

<
Brightly colored and fanciful furniture makes this playroom a perfect place for tea time.
Courtesy of PoshTots.com

Imaginations can run wild in a playroom painted to look like a city street. Here a little girl can play house with her dolls or pretend she's having tea in a fancy café.
Courtesy of Bonnie Pressley and Interiors by Decorating Den

David Van Scott Photography

David Van Scott Photography

A spare room in the house was used for a young girl's playroom. Curtains pull back to reveal a cabinet mural painted on the wall. Hanging shelves create a unique storage space for books and other odds and ends, and a window seat offers a cozy place to curl up with a favorite toy. *Courtesy of Hillner-Browne Interior Design, L.L.C.*

Bathrooms

Children fancy themselves at the shore while splashing in the bathtub, surrounded by beach-inspired wallpaper. The blue and yellow color scheme is soft and refreshing. *From the Growing Up with Waverly® Collection*

<

Dragonflies on a yellow background brighten this bathroom, which is fun for kids of any age. *From the Waverly® Storytime II Collection*

Nautical adventures are inspired by this bathroom's shower curtain and wallpaper border. *From the Waverly Storytime II Collection*

A day by the pond is the theme of this bathroom. Siblings can share this room – a mural with plants and outdoor scenery make the perfect setting for a boy, while the lily pads and the water sprite would certainly appeal to a girl. *Courtesy of Buena Vista Faux & Mural Painting*

A chest of drawers in a bathroom is great place to keep towels and other necessities. *Courtesy Young America®, A Division of Stanley Furniture Company, Inc.*

Brightly colored tropical fish are a popular decoration for any child's bathroom. They're especially fun as drawer pulls. *Courtesy of Eisenhart® Wallcoverings Co.*

Photography by Dave Parlett

Photography by Dave Parlett

Photography by Dave Parlett

B is for Bathroom, and that's not the only thing that begins with B in this room. The "B" theme extends to the ceiling, the floor, and to a mural on the wall. This bathroom incorporates an alphabet lesson into its décor. *Courtesy of Pat O'Brien*

Resource Guide

Aubergine Home Collection, Inc.
502 King Street, 2nd Floor
Charleston, SC 29403
(843) 722-3838
www.auberginehome.com

BNK Design Consultants
200 Barr Harbor Drive
Conshohocken, PA 19428
(610) 941-2943
www.bnkdesign.net

Bambini Design
82 Boylston St.
Brookline, MA 02445
(617) 730-4114

Bassett Furniture
P.O. Box 626
Bassett, Virginia 24055
(276) 629-6000
www.bassettfurniture.com

Beverly Taylor Design
11004 Holkham Court
Raleigh, NC 27614
(919) 414-4149
www.beverlytaylordesign.com

Bonavita Furniture
257 Prospect Plains Road
Cranbury, NJ 08512
1-888-266-2848
www.bonavita-cribs.com

Buena Vista Faux & Mural Painting
P.O. Box 320553
Los Gatos, California 95032
(408) 298-7531
www.bvartists.com

Christian Huebner Interiors, Inc.
15 North Ellsworth Avenue
San Mateo, CA 94401
(650) 558-8700
www.huebnerinteriors.com

Diane Boyer Interiors
A Division of Bill Behrle Associates
271 Grove Ave
Verona, NJ 07044
(973) 239-4900
www.dianeboyer.com

Eisenhart® Wallcoverings Co.
1649 Broadway
Hanover, PA 17331
1-800-931-9255
www.eisenwalls.com

Evelyn Benatar Interior Design
Great Neck, NY
(516) 482-4787
www.nyinteriordesign.com

FSC Wallcoverings
79 Madison Avenue
New York, NY 10016-7802
(212) 213-7900
www.fschumacher.com

Fashion Kids
Legget & Platt
5950 West 51st Street
Chicago IL, 60638
(708) 458-1800

Gautier USA, Inc
3155 North Andrews Avenue Extension
Pompano Beach, FL 33064
1-800-793-6075
www.gautierusa.com

Hanover Company Store, L.L.C. on behalf of Company Kids®
1500 Harbor Boulevard
Weehawken , NJ 07086
1-800-323-8000
www.companykids.com

Hillner-Browne Interior Design, L.L.C.
1095 Mount Kemble Avenue
Morristown, NJ 07960
(973) 425-1901
www.hillnerbrowne.com

Interiors by Decorating Den
1-800-DEC-DENS
www.decoratingden.com

Jan Kyle Design
4946 Belinder Rd.
Westwood, KS 66205
(913) 677-3290
www.jankyledesign.tripod.com

KAT Interiors Group, Inc.
28 Division St.
Somerville, NJ 08876
(908) 252-1881

KooKoo Bear Kids
42A Oak Street
Roswell, GA 30075
1-800-475-6909
www.kookoobearkids.com

Lark Interiors
27 Wistar Rd.
Paoli, PA 19301
(610) 889-9981
www.larkinteriors.com

Lexington Home Brands
P.O. Box 1008
Lexington NC 27293-1008
(800) 539-4636
www.lexington.com

Lisa Johnson, ASID
1624 N. West Bayshore Dr.
Suttons Bay, MI 49682
414-403-4100
www.lisainteriordesigns.com

Maine Cottage Furniture, Inc.
247 Portland Street Bldg. C
Yarmouth Maine, 04096-8130
www.mainecottage.com

Moosehead Mfg. Co
5 East Main Street
Dover-Foxcroft, ME 04426
(207) 997-3621

One Step Ahead
75 Albrecht Drive
Lake Bluff, IL 60044

Pat O'Brien
P.O. Box 1071
Cockeysville, MD 21030
(410) 303-0233
www.bestmuralist.com

PatchKraft®
70 Outwater Lane
Garfield, NJ 07026
1-800-866-2229
www.patchkraft.com

PoshTots.com
4501 Highwoods Pkwy. Ste. 200
Glen Allen, VA 23060
(866) 767-4868
www.poshtots.com

Theresa Russel Interiors
19903 Villa Lante Place
Boca Raton, FL 33434
(561) 852-0620

Thibaut®
480 Frelinghuysen Avenue
Newark, NJ 07114
(973) 643-1118
www.thibautdesign.com

Young America®
A Division of Stanley Furniture Company, Inc.
P.O. Box 30
Stanleytown, Virginia 34168
(276) 627-2245
www.youngamerica.com